HOW TO SURVIVE BIRD FLU

HOW TO SURVIVE BIRD FLU

A PRACTICAL GUIDE

DR. ANNE ROONEY

Capella

This edition published in 2006 by Arcturus Publishing Limited
26/27 Bickels Yard, 151–153 Bermondsey Street,
London SE1 3HA

In Canada published for Indigo Books
468 King St W,
Suite 500,
Toronto,
Ontario M5V 1L8

ISBN-13: 978-1-84193-473-0
ISBN-10: 1-84193-473-9

Printed in China

CONTENTS

PREFACE

As a result of concern about the H5N1 virus there has been a lot of publicity about how severe a flu pandemic might be, but very little information about how likely a severe pandemic is to occur. Pandemic flu is a real risk, but it should be kept in perspective. This book provides some much-needed background information about how pandemics occur, together with practical information about things you can do to minimize your own risk. The overall message it provides – 'Plan, don't panic' – is the right one for dealing with a risk that has a small chance of causing a really bad outcome.

H5N1 is just one of many different types of flu virus found in species of domesticated animals. A small number of people catch viral infections from animals every year and H5N1 is one of several types of bird flu, swine flu, dog and cat flu that are occasionally caught by humans. Although very large numbers of people have probably been in contact with birds carrying H5N1, only a very small number of people have been infected, but those that do get infected are made very ill and a high percentage die. Fortunately the chances of anyone catching H5N1 from contact with birds is extremely remote, and mainly restricted to people who live in intimate contact with their chickens and ducks.

If H5N1 were to mutate to become transmissible between humans then it would become a very different virus to the one we have seen being caught from direct contact with infected birds. It could happen if a person was infected with a normal transmissible flu at the same time as being infected with H5N1 and, as a result, a new cross-breed emerged. This cross-breed, like a child born from two parents, would have its own characteristics. We won't know how closely it resembles the deadly H5N1 virus until we see it. But it is actually more likely that the cross-breed will have characteristics closer to normal flu than to the H5N1 caught from birds – in order to spread easily between people it will probably become far less lethal.

If the next pandemic does arise from the H5N1 virus in one way or another, then it will no doubt still be referred to as 'Avian Flu' by the media. The transmissible form of the virus is, however, likely to be very different from the one that has dominated the media headlines to date.

In planning for any future pandemic there are important ways to minimize the risk to yourself, your family and your friends. This book sets out the important steps for protecting yourself. Inform yourself about it. Make reasonable preparations in case it happens in the next few years. Plan – don't panic.

Andrew Coburn M.A.; Dip.Arch.; Ph.D.
Vice President, Catastrophe Research
Risk Management Solutions, Inc.

Andrew Coburn is a senior executive with Risk Management Solutions (RMS) and is the chief architect of the RMS Pandemic Influenza Risk Model used by leading insurance companies to assess financial risk.

APOCALYPSE NOW?

I had a little bird,
Its name was Enza.
I opened the window,
And in-flu-enza
(1918 children's rhyme)

Might you catch bird flu this year, next year, or in five years' time? Or is it all scare-mongering to sell newspapers, flu remedies and bird flu masks? Could you suffer just a fever and a few sniffles, or might millions of people die? There are many questions that can't be answered yet with any certainty – but evidence from the past, from mathematical models and from medical science can help us make an intelligent assessment of the possibilities.

At the moment, bird flu is not a risk to most people. It is important to be clear about the distinction between:

- bird flu (H5N1), which is sometimes caught by people directly from birds
- a human form of bird flu that may evolve in the future, which could be passed directly between people.

The unknown is always more frightening than a known enemy. Although we can't answer some of the central questions about a pandemic form of bird flu until – or unless – it happens, finding out about the current situation and future threat can put them in perspective. This book addresses some common concerns, including:

- What might happen if there is a pandemic of flu from birds?
- How bad can it be?
- What might it be like?
- What can you do to protect yourself and your family?
- How can you make life most comfortable for yourself and your family during a pandemic?

Back to basics

'Bird flu' is the popular name for a flu virus that scientists label H5N1. It is currently a disease of birds, though it can occasionally be transmitted to people and some other mammals.

WHAT WE KNOW

Many wild birds carry the H5N1 virus in their intestines normally and suffer no ill effects from it.

- ✓ In some types of birds – particularly domesticated chickens, ducks and turkeys – the virus can spread quickly and cause severe illness and death.
- ✓ Some people who have been in extended, close contact with live or dead poultry infected with H5N1 have contracted bird flu.
- ✓ In humans, H5N1 can cause very serious disease and often death.
- ✓ In only a very few cases, bird flu may have been transmitted from one person to another.
- ✓ There is no threat of the current form of H5N1 spreading between people and causing a widespread epidemic (a pandemic).

WHAT WE DON'T KNOW

- ✓ If, or when, a form of bird flu transmissible between people will emerge.
- ✓ What the symptoms and effects of a transmissible form will be.
- ✓ How many people it will infect and how many it might kill.
- ✓ Whether we will have effective medicines to fight and treat it.

Although bird flu is not a danger to most people at the moment, scientists are concerned that the virus may change, by mutating, so that it can be passed easily between people. There are many flu viruses that already pass between people, and cause illnesses with effects ranging from inconvenient to fatal. The effects often depend on an individual's state of health at the time they contract flu. For bird flu to become a serious problem for people it would need to:

- change so that it can easily be passed from one person to another
- produce dangerous effects in people who are infected
- spread widely and quickly from the area or areas in which it first emerges to cause a pandemic.

The most worrying scenario would be a virus that develops and spreads quickly, giving little time for scientists to develop suitable vaccines to prevent it or drugs to treat it, and that has a high mortality rate (kills a lot of people). This may happen tomorrow, it may happen next year, or it may never happen. Many people feel they would like to be as well prepared as possible in case it does happen.

'Everyone who is knowledgeable about this will say the pandemic is inevitable. We know the pandemic clock is ticking. We just don't know what time it is.'

Dr David Fedson, retired medical director of Sanofi-Aventis

MEET THE ENEMY

Seasonal flu comes round every winter and for most people it is debilitating for a short period and then quickly forgotten. It is characterized by aching muscles, headache, fever, dry cough and a sore throat. Although you may be able to relieve the symptoms, there is no effective treatment for flu itself – you just have to wait it out. Antibiotics certainly don't help, as they treat only bacterial infections and flu is caused by a virus. For young children or elderly people, people with respiratory complaints or compromised immunity, flu can be much more dangerous. Ordinary flu kills around 36,000 people in the US and more than 12,000 people in the UK in a typical winter, with most deaths resulting from complications such as pneumonia and bronchitis.

Although seasonal flu is a familiar and regular visitor, every now and then a new, unfamiliar form of flu emerges. It can sweep around the world in months, making millions of people ill. Sometimes, it is also much more dangerous than ordinary flu, but not always.

People and pandemics

Plagues and pandemics are nothing new. Humankind has been subject to scourges and disasters throughout history and prehistory and no doubt will be for many centuries or millennia to come. Flu pandemics happen several times a century, at irregular intervals.

Pandemics and epidemics

An epidemic is the sudden occurrence of many cases of a particular illness. It becomes a pandemic if it stretches over more than one continent (from the Greek *pan*, meaning 'all', and *demos*, meaning 'people'). Pandemics occur when a lot of people are susceptible to a disease and their bodies have no resistance to it. A pandemic can happen when:

- a disease is introduced to a population with no previous exposure to it, and so no natural immunity. This happened in North and South America when Europeans introduced new diseases such as flu, measles and smallpox in the 15th and 16th centuries. These unfamiliar illnesses quickly wiped out much of the local population.

- a completely new disease appears, usually from genetic changes in an existing disease that make it unrecognizable to the human immune system. This is how flu attacks every year, and sometimes produces pandemics.
- an old disease re-emerges. After one pandemic outbreak, survivors have resistance to the disease so it cannot return with the same ferocity until immunity has diminished, but it can spread again when a sizeable susceptible population builds up.

A new disease can become a pandemic more easily than an existing disease as more people are susceptible. Our ability to fight a disease, either with medicines or by restricting the movement of people to halt its spread, can determine whether an epidemic becomes a pandemic.

An epidemic that begins in an isolated community may never spread beyond its origins. There may have been many new diseases in the past that we have never discovered because they did not escape from the areas where they originated. With modern levels of population and international travel, though, the spread of diseases can be very rapid. We can still sometimes halt an epidemic in its tracks with fast and effective management. SARS was stopped in 2003 after it spread from China to Canada.

HISTORIC PLAGUES AND PANDEMICS

1350 BCE	Egypt	Smallpox	First recorded epidemic of an identifiable disease
430 BCE	Ethiopia, Egypt, Libya, Greece	Unknown	An unknown disease wiped out 40 per cent of Athens. Symptoms were sneezing, coughing, diarrhoea, vomiting and spasms, and then rashes of ulcers and pustules and a terrible thirst
165–180; 189 CE Antonine plague	Roman Empire	Smallpox	Symptoms included fever, diarrhoea and a pustular or dry rash. Modern historians suspect that it was smallpox or

			perhaps measles. Around 5 million people died
251–66?	Roman Empire	Smallpox	Another outbreak killed up to 5,000 people a day in Rome
541–42; 588 Plague of Justinian	Middle East and Europe		The first recorded pandemic. At its height, 10,000 people a day died in Constantinople (now Istanbul), and 40 per cent of the population overall. Around 50 per cent of the population of Europe and the Middle East probably died, 25 million people
1347–48	Asia, Europe	Bubonic plague and variants	The Black Death, the second pandemic. It killed up to 40% of the population of Europe. Plague recurred over 300 years, claiming around 137 million lives between 1348 and 1700
1485–1800	North and South America	Smallpox, measles, flu	Introduced by European explorers and settlers, smallpox and other diseases devastated indigenous populations, killing up to 90 per cent of them and annihilating entire villages
1817–	India, Russia, Asia, Europe, North America	Cholera	Six cholera pandemics occurred in the 19th century and one started in 1961 in Indonesia. The worst was in 1826–37. The discovery of its spread through contaminated water during the fifth pandemic reduced the impact on industrialized nations thereafter
1855–1950	Far East, India, US,	Bubonic plague	The third pandemic spread slowly from China and its progress was eventually

	South America, Russia		challenged when the bacterium was identified and treatments developed
			Over 12 million people died.
1918–19	Worldwide	Spanish flu	Starting in France or the US, it spread around the world in several waves killing between 25 and 100 million people

Other diseases that have caused serious epidemics include typhus, polio, measles and diphtheria.

Superstition v. science

Before people understood how diseases appeared and spread, they looked for supernatural explanations for the terrors that visited from time to time. They blamed their gods, or particular groups of people (such as Roma or Jews), evil spirits, 'bad humours' or 'bad air'. They tried to appease angry gods or spirits with prayers or sacrifices or by changing their behaviour.

In the western world, most of us turn to science rather than blaming gods or evil spirits for causing disease, though when a Thai girl and her mother died of bird flu in 2003 villagers begged the local monks to exorcise the evil spirits that they believed had brought the disease.

> 'There came ... a deadly pestilence... either because of the operations of the heavenly bodies, or because of the just wrath of God mandating punishment for our iniquitous ways.'
> *Giovanni Boccaccio on the Black Death of 1346–48*

Lessons from history

> 'People in good health were all of a sudden attacked by violent heats in the head, and redness and inflammation in the eyes, the inward parts, such as the throat or tongue, becoming bloody and emitting an unnatural and fetid breath.'
> *Thucydides on the unidentified plague of 430 BCE*

The worst pandemic in history was the Black Death – a plague that ravaged the world from the 1340s to 1350 and apparently recurred at intervals of ten to thirty years for two and a half centuries.

Like any modern pandemic, it was spread by people moving around the world. Beginning in the Far East, it spread across Asia and followed trade routes to Europe, probably arriving in Italy through the port of Genoa in 1346. It took several years to run its course around the world only because it was restricted by the slow speeds at which people could travel, by boat or on foot or horseback.

Historically, the Black Death has been identified as bubonic plague and its variants, pneumonic and septicaemic plague, and many historians still hold this view. But recent studies have suggested that the Black Death could have been one or more other diseases, and perhaps a viral, haemorrhagic fever such as the Ebola fever. The jury is still out on what the Black Death really was – but there is no doubt about its catastrophic effects.

'The condition of the people was pitiable to behold. They sickened by the thousands daily, and died unattended and without help. Many died in the open street, others dying in their houses, made it known by the stench of their rotting bodies. Consecrated churchyards did not suffice for the burial of the vast multitude of bodies, which were heaped by the hundreds in vast trenches, like goods in a ship's hold and covered with a little earth.'

Giovanni Boccaccio on the Black Death of 1346–48

Social chaos

The horrors related by chroniclers of early plagues don't end with the diseases, terrible enough in themselves. It's hard to imagine the social effects caused by nearly half of the population dying.

'Work of every description ceased, and all the trades were abandoned by the artisans, and all other work as well, such as each had in hand. Indeed in a city which was simply abounding in all good things starvation almost absolute was running riot.'

Procopius on the Plague of Justinian, 541 BCE

The effects were disastrous. After the first pandemic in 541–542, the whole of Europe fell into a decline which lasted for centuries. Eight hundred years later, the Black Death wiped out farming communities, leading to famine throughout Europe while crops rotted in the fields. Between 25 per cent and 50 per cent of the population died; in some areas, whole villages or towns were wiped out. Suddenly, labourers and peasants who had endured a hand-to-mouth existence on subsistence wages were able to command huge salaries, holding the landowners to ransom. Revolts and rebellions around Europe ensued and the whole structure of society changed.

> 'After the pestilence, many buildings, great and small, fell into ruins in every city for lack of inhabitants, likewise many villages and hamlets became desolate, not a house being left in them, all having died who dwelt there; and it was probable that many such villages would never be inhabited.'
>
> *Henry Knighton on the Black Death of 1346–48*

Some people fear that bird flu could again lead to such an apocalyptic scenario. But both the world and the diseases are very different now.

Why bird flu is not the Black Death

There has never been a strain of flu which has killed at the rate that the Black Death did, or has even come remotely close to it. With more than half the infected people dying, the Black Death took a truly terrible toll. Even the most deadly flu pandemic, which circled the world in 1918, claimed only 2.5 per cent of those infected (in industrialized western societies) while the Black Death killed at least 50 per cent of infected people.

Some of the symptoms of the Black Death look alarmingly similar to those of 1918 flu. Flu victims suffered terrible fever, and many turned blue or purple in the face as they were starved of oxygen by lung damage. Some died very rapidly, seemingly quite well in the morning and dead by evening. Chroniclers of the Black Death wrote of people suffering raging fever, coughing up blood, turning a dark shade of purple or black and dying within hours of falling ill. But these symptoms can be caused by many different illnesses, and there is no suggestion that the Black Death was a form of flu. If it was bubonic plague and its variants, that is caused by a bacterium, *Yesinia pestis*. If it was a haemorrhagic fever, like Ebola, it could have been caused by one of a number of viruses, but none of them is related to the flu viruses at all.

The Black Death struck at a time when people had practically no understanding of how illness spread or affected the body. Some of the medical treatments they tried made the situation worse rather than better. Their best shot at stemming the pandemic was quarantine – nothing else they tried had any beneficial effect. Nowadays, we have many medical interventions to help people, and can use antibiotics to treat bacterial infections such as bubonic plague. Although another Black Death is not impossible, it is very unlikely – and flu is certainly not likely to be the trigger.

> 'Neither physicians nor medicines were effective. Whether because these illnesses were previously unknown or because physicians had not previously studied them, there seemed to be no cure. There was such a fear that no one seemed to know what to do.'
> *Marchione di Coppo Stefani, on the Black Death*

Last time round: 1918

There are generally three or four flu pandemics in a century. The most devastating occurred nearly ninety years ago and is often the benchmark against which the threat of a new pandemic is measured.

In 1918 a terrifying flu pandemic swept the whole world, killing more people than any other pandemic before it. It was unlike any flu previously recorded and claimed more victims than the First Word War, which was just ending as flu took hold. (The Black Death killed a higher proportion of the population than flu, but the much greater size of the population in 1918 meant that the numbers killed in the flu pandemic dwarfed the total killed by plague. Had the Black Death struck the population of 1918, it would have killed nearly 500 million, whereas flu killed around a tenth of that number.)

TIMELINE – 1918

Winter 1916/17	Deadly, flu-like virus emerges in Etaples, an army station in northern France. Up to 100,000 soldiers mix freely and buy live chickens, geese and turkeys from French markets. The virus begins like flu, but victims later turn purple in the face and die, coughing up blood. This might have been the origin of the 1918 flu virus
Winter 1917/1918	Coldest winter on record in some areas of the US; epidemic pneumonia kills many soldiers living in cramped camp conditions. Another possibility is that the 1918 flu virus emerged during this winter in Haskell, Kansas
Spring 1918	First wave: influenza outbreaks in Fort Riley, Kansas, US, and then in other army camps around the US, go largely unnoticed. On the first day in Fort Riley, 100 men report sick by lunchtime
Late August 1918	Sailors stationed in Boston, US, start falling sick with flu
September 1918	Second wave: simultaneous outbreaks of deadly flu in Freetown, South Africa; Kentucky, US; and in France. These spread rapidly to all areas
October 1918	195,000 Americans die of flu; pandemic at its height in many parts of the world; Inuit communities hit very hard, with up to 50 per cent mortality
November 1918	Second wave of pandemic recedes and is over in most places by the end of the month
December 1918	Third wave of pandemic, less virulent; flu reaches Australia
January 1919	Third wave peaks in US
February 1919	Third wave peaks in Europe
Winter 1919/1920	Flu returns; in eight weeks 11,000 people die in New York City and Chicago; flu deaths in 1920 are the second or third highest of the 20th century

Not an ordinary flu

Many people infected in 1918 suffered no more than a bad bout of flu with fever, aching muscles and headaches. But for others the symptoms and outcomes were terrible and terrifying:

- extreme difficulty breathing
- coughing so hard that some people tore chest muscles
- lungs flooded with blood and fluid, causing coughing and suffocation
- heliotrope cyanosis – the face turns purple as the blood contains no oxygen
- multiple organ failure
- bronchitis and (bacterial) pneumonia
- long-term depression and mood changes
- lasting lung or brain damage
- death.

CYTOKINE STORM –
WHEN THE BODY TURNS ON ITSELF

Doctors treating flu patients in 1918 were puzzled at the extremely vicious reactions and gruesome deaths they witnessed. They described it as a severe pneumonia, but medical historians suggest that it may have been a 'cytokine storm' response. This happens when the body's immune system goes into overdrive, but cannot identify the enemy. It ends up flooding the body with white blood cells, wreaking terrible damage. The white blood cells release proteins called cytokines that call more white blood cells and a loop is set up. The lungs clog with cells and can't absorb oxygen. A completely new virus unrecognized by the immune system can cause this overload of cytokines.

Many of the human victims of H5N1 have also suffered a cytokine storm response which has often been fatal, even with advanced hospital care.

Bodies 'stacked like cordwood'

The 1918 pandemic infected up to half of the world's population. In the US, 2.5 per cent of infected people died, with half of those being aged 20–40.

> 'These men start with what appears to be an ordinary attack of *la grippe* or influenza, and when brought to the hosp. they very rapidly develop the most viscous [sic] type of pneumonia that has ever been seen. Two hours after admission they have the Mahogany spots over the cheek bones, and a few hours later you can begin to see the cyanosis extending from their ears and spreading all over the face, until it is hard to distinguish the coloured men from the white. It is only a matter of a few hours then until death comes, and it is simply a struggle for air until they suffocate. It is horrible. One can stand it to see one, two or twenty men die, but to see these poor devils dropping like flies sort of gets on your nerves. We have been averaging about 100 deaths per day, and still keeping it up... For several days there were no coffins and the bodies piled up something fierce, we used to go down to the morgue (which is just [at the] back of my ward) and look at the boys laid out in long rows. It beats any sight they ever had in France after a battle.'
>
> *Letter from Dr T Francis, army doctor based in Boston, September 1918*

Death figures for the 1918 pandemic are hard to pin down, especially as much of Asia and Africa did not collect statistics. Estimates have been revised recently, with new figures substantially higher than the originals. Even these figures are only estimates.

Region	**1927 figures**	**2002 figures**
India	12.5 million	18.5 million
Europe	2.16 million	2.3 million
US	550,000	680,000
Total worldwide	21.64 million	48.8–100 million

Total world population in 1918 = approx. 1.8 billion

Amongst the worst-hit countries were India and Iran, where malaria, poverty, famine and other diseases made the impact of flu far worse. Up to 50 per cent or even 60 per cent of the population died in some places. India alone accounted for 60 per cent of all reported flu deaths in the world.

> 'I saw hundreds of young stalwart men in uniform coming into the wards of the hospital. Every bed was full, yet others crowded in. The faces wore a bluish cast; a cough brought up the blood-stained sputum. In the morning, the dead bodies are stacked about the morgue like cordwood.'
>
> *Dr Victor Vaughan, acting Surgeon General of the US Army on a visit to Camp Devens, Boston in September 1918; 63 men died the day of his visit*

The 1918 flu virus infected up to half of the world's population and killed 50 times as many of its victims as normal, seasonal flu. Working out why its effects were so extreme is key to understanding the effects a future flu pandemic may have.

THE 1918 VIRUS AND BIRD FLU

Using samples of lung tissue preserved in an Eskimo victim of 1918 flu buried in the permafrost, scientists have managed to sequence the genetic code of the strain and recreate it in the laboratory. The full genetic sequence was published in October 2005.

They found that the 1918 flu evolved entirely from a strain of bird flu and did not combine with a human strain. After infecting mice with the virus, they discovered that it was far more virulent than they had expected – after four days it had created 39,000 times as much virus as a modern strain of flu would do. They hope that understanding the exact structure of the 1918 flu strain will help to identify changes in H5N1 which may lead to its becoming transmissible between people. They believe that so far H5N1 has acquired half of the ten genetic changes needed to become transmissible between humans.

In analyzing the 1918 strain, scientists discovered a protein inside the virus which matches one found in strains of H5N1 that have killed people in the Far East, and found also in a strain of H7N7 (another flu virus) which killed a man in the Netherlands (see p36).

Young, healthy people died more often than children or older people in the 1918 pandemic. This is exactly what would be expected of a cytokine storm response (extreme immune system reaction), as the people with the most robust immune system will be able to inflict the most damage on themselves. Although infection rates were highest amongst children, mortality rates were lowest – they have weak immune systems.

There is no reason to suspect that the next flu pandemic will be as terrible in its effects as that of 1918. There have been reports of flu epidemics and pandemics since 1580, and none has approached the devastation of 1918.

Fear

> 'A fear and panic of the influenza, akin to the terror of the Middle Ages regarding the Black Plague, [has] been prevalent in many parts of the country.'
> *American Red Cross report, 1918 flu*

The 1918 pandemic was little understood and badly managed by governments and health authorities. Information was withheld from the public, increasing fear to the point where panic was almost as dangerous as the disease. People refused to nurse victims, sick people were shunned and both the ill and orphaned children were left to starve in their houses. It is a pattern that had been seen in pandemics centuries before. It is one we can hope not to repeat in the future.

Flu before 1918

The earliest recorded flu pandemic was in 1580 and some medical historians have suggested that the human flu viruses are only 500 years old. (There are some earlier accounts of diseases that may or may not have been flu.)

FLU PANDEMICS

1580	First confirmed flu pandemic; started in Asia Minor (Turkey) and North Africa in 1580, then infected Europe (through Italy) and ultimately America, where over 90 per cent of the populace was afflicted. Mortality was extremely high, not helped by doctors treating the disease by bleeding patients
1729–30	Thought to originate in Russia, and spread throughout Europe. High infection levels but low mortality; most deaths were amongst the elderly and pregnant women
1732–33	First global pandemic; reported to affect dogs and horses as well as people
1781–82	Global pandemic originating in Asia; mortality high amongst elderly people; tens of millions of cases
1830–31	Global pandemic originating in China; very high infection rates (up to 80 per cent in some areas), low death rates except amongst the elderly and people with respiratory complaints
1833	Russia and Europe
1836–37	Global pandemic, possibly related to the 1833 strain. Very high infection rate; 2–2.5 per cent of infected people died, many deaths associated with pneumonia
1889–90	First well documented global pandemic; infection rates were around 50 per cent, with case mortality probably 0.2 per cent; later waves in following years had a higher death rate

Flu since 1918

Two further flu pandemics since 1918 have had serious, but less catastrophic, effects. Other epidemics or scares have caused fewer problems.

- **1957:** Asian flu originating in the Far East was identified in February and became a pandemic in the winter of 1957–58, sweeping the world in two waves. A vaccine was developed in 1958. Two million people died.

- **1968–69:** Hong Kong flu emerged early in the year and became a pandemic in the winter of 1968–69. It recurred in 1970 and 1972. Most of the three quarters of a million deaths were amongst elderly people. It was related to the Asian flu of 1957, and so some people already had immunity.
- **1976:** A scare over so-called swine flu, which was thought to be related to the 1918 strain, launched a mass vaccination programme in the US, but the virus did not spread beyond its origins in New Jersey. The vaccination programme became a tragic fiasco, with ten people dying from the vaccine, and seriously undermined the chance of the US preparing properly for a future pandemic.
- **1977:** Russian flu spread around the world. It affected mainly young people and children who had no immunity to the type of flu common before 1957 and was rarely fatal.

Near misses?

The threat of a terrible epidemic is kept alive for us all by Hollywood, by half-remembered school studies of the Black Death and by occasional scares around the world. Besides the lesser flu pandemics, recent years have seen Ebola fever, Marburg fever, SARS and HIV/AIDS. Of these, only HIV/AIDS has turned into a genuine pandemic, yet its slow onset and the difficulty of transmission means that it doesn't generate panic in the general population.

EBOLA

Description	Haemorrhagic fever
Origins	Democratic Republic of Congo (Zaire), Africa, 1976
Symptoms	Fever, malaise, headache, backache, vomiting, diarrhoea, haemorrhagic rash (raised spots containing blood), internal bleeding, bleeding from mouth, rectum, eyes, ears and nose, breathing difficulties, delirium, coma
Transmission	Person-to-person in body fluids and by close contact; contact with infected bodies
Mortality	50–90 per cent (different strains)
Cause	Viral; probably passed from animals (rodents, ticks, fleas)

Treatment	None effective
Vaccine	None
Deaths to date	Over 1,200 deaths of around 1,850 cases of infection

HIV/AIDS

Description	Autoimmune deficiency; the victim's immune system is disabled, making them vulnerable to all other diseases. HIV is the first stage and full-blown AIDS develops after about 10–12 years if no treatment is given. In some African countries, HIV infection rates are over 25 per cent of the population
Origins	Africa; identified 1981
Symptoms	HIV, the precursor to AIDS, is usually asymptomatic; when AIDS develops, fatigue, muscle aches and other symptoms appear, but the symptoms of the opportunistic diseases that infect an AIDS patient vary
Transmission	Body fluids (blood and semen) – sex and re-use of needles, often by drug users, are the main methods of transmission; transfusion with infected blood products occurred when the disease was emerging
Mortality	100 per cent if untreated
Cause	Viral
Treatment	Drugs to boost the immune system and delay the onset of full-blown AIDS; treatment of opportunistic conditions that develop because of low immunity
Vaccine	None
Deaths to date	Around 25 million of 65 million cases; 40.3 million currently living with HIV/AIDS

SARS (SEVERE ACUTE RESPIRATORY SYNDROME)

Description	Viral, respiratory infection commonly leading to cytokine storm
Origins	Far East, 2003
Symptoms	High fever, headache, cough, breathing difficulties, pneumonia

Transmission	Person-to-person in body fluids and by close contact; airborne droplets
Mortality	9 per cent
Cause	Corona virus (it is not related to the flu virus, but is closer to the common cold virus); thought to have originated in mammals used in medicine in China
Treatment	Oxygen to help breathing difficulties, antiviral drugs, physiotherapy to help clear lungs
Vaccine	None
Deaths to date	Over 744 of 8,098 infected

Profile of a pandemic

A pandemic is marked by a cluster of cases of an illness, rapidly spreading to more and more people. The speed of spread depends on many factors including:

- how long people can pass on the disease before they become very ill (ill people typically have contact with few others)
- how easily the disease spreads between people
- how long people stay infectious after recovery.

A pandemic peaks when the rate at which sick people can spread it drops off, either because many people have already had the disease (or been vaccinated against it) and are immune, or because movements are so restricted that few people come into contact with it. A second wave of a pandemic may occur if the disease changes enough for immunity to the earlier strain to be no protection. The pandemic dies down when very few susceptible people come into contact with the disease.

Between pandemics, the virus or bacterium survives in a reservoir that may be a group of people or another species that is not made ill by the disease. When an outbreak starts, the first traceable human case – the index case or 'patient zero' – forms a pathway for the infection of other people. Tracing the index case helps epidemiologists to understand how the disease is transmitted and what its reservoir may be.

S, I, R

Pandemic models divide the part of the population involved in a pandemic into three groups:

- **S** = susceptible – people who have no immunity and may become infected
- **I** = infected
- **R** = recovered

Some people may be naturally immune, or have acquired imunity either in a previous outbreak or through vaccination. In statistical models, people who have developed immunity are shown to be important in constraining the spread of a disease.

THE NEXT PANDEMIC?

No one doubts that sooner or later another pandemic will strike the world. The billion-dollar questions are – What it will be? When will it emerge? How dangerous it will be? Currently, many experts fear that bird flu could produce the next one. Huge international effort is going into tracking H5N1 in the bird population and exploring the virus and its variants. We cannot know before it happens whether bird flu will produce a pandemic, but by investing money and energy into preparing to meet the threat we can hope to minimize its effects if it does happen. Opinion about the likelihood of a bird flu pandemic is divided, even amongst world experts on flu and pandemic diseases.

> 'Most experts believe that it is not a question of whether there will be another severe influenza pandemic, but when.'
> *Sir Liam Donaldson, UK Chief Medical Officer, 2002*

Bugs and birds

The flu variant H5N1 is a disease found primarily in birds, though it occasionally transfers to other animals. At the moment, it does not spread readily between people. There has been one confirmed case of this happening, and a few more cases in which it might have happened. If the disease remains restricted mostly to birds, it will not become a human pandemic. Even so, it will have a terrible impact on the people around the world who depend on farming poultry for a living. This is part of the problem – farmers may be reluctant to reveal cases, and government authorities reluctant to admit it is in flocks on their territory, because of the dire financial consequences of having to kill their chickens. When people avoid action for these reasons, the disease can spread unhindered, and then the chance of it changing enough to become transmissible between people is increased.

Sick birds

In domestic poultry, H5N1 infects every part of the body and causes bleeding from all organs and the skin. The birds fall sick quickly and can die in 48 hours. The disease generally kills 100 per cent of an infected flock of chickens, so it's not difficult to spot. If birds are kept in high densities, as they often are on modern farms, disease spreads very quickly amongst them.

Although it is easy to detect bird flu in an infected flock, the consequences of reporting infection are devastating. In some parts of the world, poultry farmers receive little or no compensation for culled birds and so may not be quick to notify authorities. There are reports of bird flu being hidden in parts of the Far East and of huge, industrial chicken farmers avoiding culling their flocks even when small domestic producers were losing theirs.

Human victims

Although there are probably millions of birds infected with bird flu, there have been remarkably few human infections. Between 2003 and the end of April 2006 205 reported cases of bird flu in people resulted in 113 deaths (56 per cent). Almost all of these people had been infected by handling infected birds or being exposed to bird faeces. For most of us, who do not handle birds on a daily basis and are unlikely to come into contact with an infected bird, the risk of catching bird flu is extremely small. But the dire consequences of infection for the unlucky few has made the prospect of bird flu terrifying.

BIRD FLU TIMELINE

1878	Symptoms first identified in birds
1955	Identified as a flu virus
1959	H5N1 strain isolated; discovered in a chicken in Scotland
1983	Outbreak of H5N2 in Pennsylvania, US; 20 million poultry culled
1991	Outbreak of H5N1 on an English turkey farm
1996	H5N1 discovered in a farmed goose in Guangdong province, China
March 1997	Chickens on a farm near the Mai Po marshes in Hong Kong start dying; chickens culled
May 1997	In the first human case of H5N1 infection, a three-year-old boy dies of respiratory and organ failure
December 1997	More human cases in Hong Kong – 5 of 17 cases

	are fatal; all 1.6 million poultry in Hong Kong slaughtered; import of live birds from mainland China banned; city's markets disinfected
1998	H5N1 and many other flu viruses found in Chinese poultry flocks
Spring 2002	Industrial chicken farming in California hit by H6N2 flu virus, which spread to other regions; outbreak hushed up to protect commercial interests
December 2002	Wild birds including ducks, geese and flamingos die of bird flu in Hong Kong's parks
February 2003	One fatal human case of H5N1 in Hong Kong, one person recovers and another fatality may have been a victim of H5N1 but was not tested; SARS outbreak starts; H7N7 bird flu in the Netherlands results in culling of 30 million chickens and one human death
November 2003	H5N1 epidemic in chickens in Thailand, but authorities fail to respond; giant chicken producers, CP, accused of a cover-up as they apparently process and export diseased chicken and are exempt from culling
December 2003	Two tigers and two leopards die of H5N1 after eating infected raw chickens
January – March 2004	Fatal human cases in Vietnam; H5N1 reported in poultry in Japan
February 2004	Fatal, atypical case of H5N1 in Vietnam in which a person had encephalitis and diarrhoea but no respiratory problems
September 2004	First human-to-human transmission of H5N1, Thailand
February 2005	A Vietnamese man who contracted H5N1 may have passed it to two other people; all recovered after treatment with Tamiflu
Spring – summer 2005	New strains of H5N1 in birds in China more dangerous to wild birds
July 2005	Civets in Vietnam die of H5N1; H5N1 found in migratory birds in Russia

October 2005	Dead wild ducks found in Romania show that H5N1 has reached Europe; H5N1 found on a turkey farm in Greece
November 2005	H5N1 found in a flamingo in Kuwait, the first instance in the Gulf States
January 2006	First human cases in Turkey and Iraq
March 2006	Human trials of a vaccine against H5 variants begin in the Netherlands; first human cases in Azerbaijan
April 2006	First case of H5N1 in the UK; a dead swan found in Scotland; outbreak of H7N3 bird flu on a chicken farm in England

Where in the world?

TRAVELLING IN AREAS WITH BIRD FLU

If you're travelling to an area where there's bird flu amongst birds, take sensible measures to protect yourself. At the moment there is no reason to avoid these areas.

Before you go –

- ✓ Check government health advice and make sure you have any necessary vaccinations – check at least six weeks before your trip
- ✓ Take basic health supplies, including a thermometer to monitor your temperature and an adequate supply of alcohol-based hand-wipes
- ✓ Make sure you have travel health insurance, and that it will cover emergency repatriation if necessary.

While you are there –

- ✓ Wash your hands frequently, and especially if you go near poultry or touch uncooked eggs or poultry. Use soap and water if possible, alcohol-based hand-wipes or gel if soap and water are not available
- ✓ Don't eat foods containing raw or undercooked eggs, such as dishes or sauces thickened with uncooked whipped eggs, cooked eggs with runny yolks or omelettes that are not set. Poultry and eggs should be cooked at temperatures of 74°C

(165°F) or above to destroy viruses. Properly cooked chicken and eggs are safe
- ✓ Don't eat undercooked poultry or uncooked blood from poultry – two people in Vietnam may have contracted H5N1 in 2005 from consuming uncooked duck blood
- ✓ Avoid poultry farms and markets where live and uncooked poultry are sold
- ✓ Don't handle dead or live poultry or wild birds
- ✓ Don't touch surfaces that might have been contaminated by bird faeces or secretions
- ✓ Don't stand too close to poultry or wild birds.

When you get home –
- ✓ Look out for any flu symptoms, such as fever, coughing, sore throat, or difficulty in breathing for ten days after your return
- ✓ If you need to seek medical attention for any of these symptoms, tell your health care provider where you have been and when, and about any contact with poultry or eggs when you make your appointment and as soon as you arrive at the health care provider's premises so that appropriate precautions can be taken
- ✓ Do not travel; minimize contact with other people while you are ill, apart from travelling to receive medical care.

There is more on what to do if you or a member of your family falls ill on pp71–73.

Why now?

If the symptoms of bird flu were first spotted in 1878 and we have known about the virus itself since 1959, why has the scare only just started?

For the bird flu virus to become transmissible between people, it needs to acquire new features that will let it target human tissue. The easiest way for this to happen is for it to combine with a human flu virus and take on some of its properties. This could come about if a person already infected with a human flu strain also caught H5N1 from a bird. At that point, the bird flu virus has a chance to mix its genes with those of the human flu virus and perhaps gain the ability to spread directly between people. The more contact between people and infected birds there is, the more likely this is to happen. This is how the pandemic flu strains of 1957 and 1968 came about. But the virus could also change without crossing with another strain. The 1918 flu is believed to have been a wholly bird-originated strain that became able to infect people easily.

ALL CHANGE

New flu strains can develop in two ways.

Antigenic drift happens when a virus makes copies of itself that are inaccurate, and the errors in the virus change its properties. These changes are generally small, so major change takes place slowly. It is the way the winter flu virus changes from year to year, and is probably the way that the 1918 flu developed.

Antigenic shift happens when much larger chunks of the virus's identity change in one go. Inside the flu virus, eight segments of genetic material, RNA, hold the information defining the virus. If two different flu viruses come together in the same infected cell, they can swap around these eight segments in a process called reassortment. The new virus may have three segments from one virus and five from the other, for example. It is so different from either separately that the immune system cannot recognize it as related. This process can produce a form of bird flu transmissible between humans, as happened in 1957 and in 1968. The reassortment could take place in a person who has caught both forms of flu, or possibly in another animal (such as a pig) which can contract both types.

Intensive farming methods and growing populations of both people and poultry make a human flu virus from birds more likely now than ever before. The chances for the virus to transfer between humans and birds is greatest in South East Asia, where people live in very close contact with their poultry. There are 700 million chickens in the Chinese province of Guangzhou and every square kilometre of the Pearl River delta is home to 1,273 people. (The Chinese poultry population has increased 1000-fold since the 1968 flu pandemic.) That makes for a lot of human–chicken contact and plenty of opportunity for humans to breathe in viruses from their birds, common in the birds' faeces.

CHILD'S PLAY?

In many parts of the world, looking after poultry is a job for children. This is probably why so many of the bird flu victims to date have been young children. Only days after the first child victims of bird flu in Turkey died, TV cameras filmed children in the same village kicking around dead chickens and playing with and hugging live chickens.

Spreading its wings

Bird flu has escaped from the intensively farmed areas of South East Asia, carried by migrating wild birds which have had contact with domestic chickens and ducks. Ducks and geese from Siberia brought H5N1 to Europe in 2005. Ducks can carry the disease without developing symptoms or falling sick. The ducks become a reservoir of the virus, which can then spread silently. It is likely that H5N1 will be endemic in wild birds in Europe in a very short time. From them, it can spread to domestic flocks, especially if they are kept outside.

It is not just migrating wild birds that can carry flu long distances. Bird smuggling and even legitimate movement of birds over borders can help the disease along. A consignment of finches imported into the UK was found to be carrying bird flu in October 2005 after a parrot died of the disease. Luckily, they had not been smuggled and the virus was discovered while they were in quarantine; all exposed birds were destroyed.

FAQS

Is it safe to visit farms and wild bird reserves in Europe?

At the moment it is safe to visit many places where you can view and even feed birds. You are unlikely to come into contact with an infected bird. Always wash your hands after feeding birds or touching surfaces they may have walked on, and do not approach a dead or sick-looking bird. Guidelines will be issued if it becomes unsafe to visit farms and wildlife reserves.

Should you feed and encourage birds in your garden?
It is safe to feed birds in your garden. There have been no recorded instances of bird flu in garden birds. Wash your hands carefully after touching any bird feeding equipment, bird baths, nesting boxes or surfaces birds use.

Is it safe to eat eggs and chicken?
Yes. Make sure they are properly cooked – this is a sensible precaution at all times. No one has contracted bird flu from eating properly cooked meat or eggs from contaminated birds. Indeed, contaminated poultry meat was probably sold in Thailand and around Asia for several months with no consumers suffering any ill effects.

Culling and containment

Hopes of stemming the tide of bird flu in its current forms rest on culling birds in affected areas and preventing infected birds moving into other areas. The first method has huge financial and social implications, especially for small-scale family farmers in poor countries; the second has been made practically impossible by the spread into wild birds, and the emergence of wild ducks as carriers who don't succumb to the disease.

Hong Kong cull

When H5N1 struck poultry in Hong Kong in 1997, a large-scale culling operation to kill all the birds in Hong Kong city and the surrounding area contained the spread of the virus, but it soon appeared on the Chinese mainland. Culls in other areas of the Far East can be more difficult. In areas of Vietnam, Cambodia, rural China and Thailand, corruption and fear of the financial implications often undermine culling programmes.

Estimates suggest that 120 million poultry had been culled in the Far East between 1997 and the early spring of 2006. In Vietnam in 2005, 46 million chickens and ducks were culled and a further 60 million vaccinated against H5N1.

'You start killing and killing and killing, and there are still thousands of birds.'
Clive Lau, agriculture official, Hong Kong

Dutch courage

Chicken farming is intensive in the Netherlands. There are 90 million chickens and a human population of 16 million, with the export of poultry and eggs worth 284 million euros a year. An outbreak of the bird flu strain H7N7 in the Netherlands in February 2003 resulted in 89 people being infected, and one death. The Dutch culled 30 million chickens and managed to contain the outbreak within four months.

Most people affected suffered only mild symptoms, but one man died from a mutated, more virulent strain of H7N7. He did not pass the strain to anyone else, but families of people exposed to the less virulent form of H7N7 did become infected without direct contact with poultry themselves.

An outbreak of H7N3 in England in April 2006 was also tackled by culling birds in the affected area.

Containment

Containment involves preventing the spread of the virus by restricting movement of infected birds. Although the movement of domestic birds can be regulated, now that the virus is widespread amongst wild birds, some of which migrate over large distances, containment is not possible. Short of killing all wild birds in areas in which H5N1 has ever been found – and even that is unlikely to be effective – there is no way of forcing the genie back into the bottle now it has escaped. Killing vast numbers of wild birds would prompt an ecological disaster which may be worse than the effects of bird flu. (When Chinese authorities tried to wipe out flies in the 1960s, the attempt had to be abandoned as birds that eat flies, and then the predators of those birds, began to die in large numbers, threatening to tip China into an ecological tail-spin from which there may have been no recovery.)

On a smaller scale, keeping poultry under cover to separate it from wild birds is being suggested in Europe and the US. Some European countries have insisted on this already. Moving all poultry indoors is not feasible in the Far East where it would mean keeping birds under the same roof as the people who farm them.

Vaccination

Vaccinating poultry against bird flu has been suggested and even used in some places. In other places it is not generally thought viable. Each chicken needs to be vaccinated by injection individually. Intensively farmed chickens are kept alive only for a few weeks, and all new poultry must be vaccinated. The administrative and financial burdens are immense.

Vaccination has other disadvantages. Although birds do not become sick, they may still harbour and spread the virus, creating a vast reservoir that could eventually do more harm than good. One way to track the spread of the virus while vaccinating is to leave a few birds unvaccinated as 'sentinels'. If the virus infected a flock, the sentinels would be affected, alerting a farmer to the problem.

A large-scale vaccination programme runs the risk of speeding up the development of strains resistant to vaccines and treatments. A misguided attempt at vaccination in China is thought to have led to the super-virulent strain of H5N1.

FAQS

Is it still safe to keep hens in the garden?

Yes. Government guidelines will be issued if it becomes necessary to keep hens indoors, but at the moment this is not required in most parts of the UK or in the US. Wash your hands carefully after handling birds or eggs and after cleaning their coops or feeding them.

Can I have my hens vaccinated?

Not at the moment. Vets are not supplying a vaccine for inoculating small flocks of chickens in the UK. The situation may change – in the UK, check the website of Defra (Department for Environment, Food and Rural Affairs, www.defra.gov.uk) for updates on keeping poultry in the garden or on a small-holding.

Should I move my hens indoors?

In areas where bird flu has been found amongst wild birds, people are advised or required to keep chickens in a covered area. However, if your hens mix with wild ducks and geese, you may prefer to segregate them or cover their enclosure as a precaution even if it is not required.

If we have to cull poultry, how will it be done?
It is likely that chickens will be culled through gassing with carbon dioxide by vets or other trained personnel. Defra will make announcements if culling becomes necessary. Culling will be required only in areas with a confirmed outbreak of bird flu.

DISEASE FROM ANIMALS
If bird flu remains confined mostly to birds, not becoming transmissible between people, it will join the ranks of many human diseases which are carried by animals, including:
Malaria: the deadliest of animal-borne diseases, it is spread by mosquitoes and caused by a parasite deposited in the blood by a mosquito bite. Between 300 and 500 million cases of malaria occur every year and more than one million people a year die of malaria.
Bubonic plague: bacterial disease spread by fleas that usually live on rodents, it has killed millions of people over the centuries but is treatable today.
Lyme disease: bacterial disease carried by ticks in Europe and the US, usually successfully treated with antibiotics.
Rabies: a viral disease in mammals, spread to people through bites from infected wild or domestic animals including racoons, skunks, dogs, bats and cattle. Fatal if not treated quickly.

What about us?

'It's very unusual that a virus with pandemic potential actually appears. So, that has us concerned from the beginning. But have we seen any change in the last two years that makes us think that this is on the edge of mutating into a pandemic strain? … Definitely not.'
Dr Dick Thompson, World Health Organization spokesman on communicable diseases

So far, there have been very few cases of H5N1 spreading directly between people and causing illness. However, antibodies to H5N1 have been found in people involved in culling and dealing with dead birds after an outbreak, and in members of their families and other close contacts. The presence of antibodies shows that they have had contact with the virus and their immune systems have responded to combat it. Some people suffered minor effects from H5N1 such as conjunctivitis (inflammation of the eyes). There is no tracking of mild cases of H5N1 infection as these do not usually come to the attention of medical workers. There may be a mild strain of H5N1 circulating in Asia and infection levels may be much higher than recognized. This could be good or bad – if a pandemic develops from a mild strain, it may be less dangerous. But if many people are infected with H5N1, the potential for a more serious strain spreading amongst people may be greater.

> 'Once a fully contagious virus emerges, its global spread is considered inevitable.'
> *WHO website*

It is still quite difficult to catch bird flu from infected birds and their faeces, so even if all wild birds became carriers the infection rate amongst people would remain relatively low. For bird flu to become pandemic, it would need to be able to spread directly between people, without the use of birds as an intermediary.

GenZ

The strain of H5N1 which has infected some people in the Far East is referred to as GenZ. It may have developed as a result of Chinese farmers secretly using a vaccine to protect their chickens after an outbreak of H5N1 in 1997.

Human cases of GenZ are resistant to standard anti-flu medicines, leaving only Relenza and Tamiflu as any kind of defence (see pp58–59). GenZ also frequently causes a cytokine storm response in human cases – the body's immune system goes into overdrive, destroying its own cells and causing a rapid, horrible death.

CASE HISTORY: PRANEE THONGCHAN

The first recorded case of probable person-to-person transmission of H5N1 was between a daughter and mother in Thailand in September 2004. Chickens began dying in the village of Ban Srisomboon from a disease which the villagers recognized as bird flu. Sakuntala Thongchan fell ill with stomachache and fever, dismissed by a nurse as a bad cold. Five days later she was vomiting blood and was admitted to hospital. Her mother, Pranee Thongchan was recalled from work near Bangkok and arrived as her daughter was dying. She spent the night cradling and soothing her daughter who died the next day. The cause of Sakuntala's death was recorded as dengue fever and the child's body was cremated without anyone taking tissue samples. Suffering from fatigue and muscle aches, Pranee was told she was exhausted and grief-stricken. She later collapsed and died in hospital two weeks after her daughter. Pranee's sister also contracted bird flu, but was successfully treated with Tamiflu and recovered.

How viruses work

Most pandemic diseases – smallpox, typhus, polio, cholera, measles, hepatitis, flu, HIV – are viral. Only diphtheria, whooping cough and bubonic plague are bacterial. Viral infections are much harder to combat than bacterial infections. They do not respond to antibiotics (which only kill bacteria). Vaccination is our best method of protecting ourselves, but we need a new vaccine for every virus.

Unlike a bacterium, a virus can't manage for long on its own – it needs a host, and can only copy itself by hijacking cells of the host's body and taking over its mechanism for making proteins.

BACTERIUM OR VIRUS?

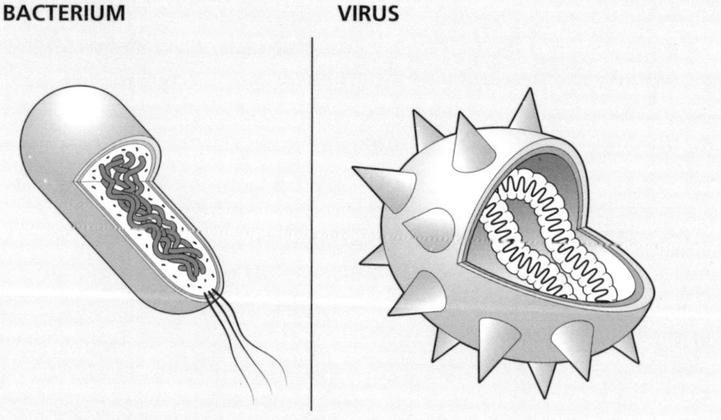

BACTERIUM OR VIRUS?

BACTERIUM	VIRUS
Living micro-organism, made of a single cell	Fragment of DNA or RNA in a coat of proteins. It is debatable whether a virus counts as a living thing or just a complex chemical
Reproduces by splitting into two, like other cells – the bacterium can reproduce on its own	Hijacks the internal mechanism in a cell to make multiple copies of itself, then bursts the cell, releasing all the copies to infect other cells
Divides in two every 20 minutes minutes – symptoms of infection typically take days to appear	When the cell bursts, thousands of viruses can be released – symptoms can appear within hours or minutes
1000 nanometres across (1 nanometre = 1 thousand-millionth of a metre)	20–250 nanometres across (the flu virus is 100 nanometres)
Combatted with antibiotics	Combatted with a cocktail of anti-viral medicines and drugs to boost the immune system to help the body make its own defences
Mutation is slow – about one in 100 million reproductions produces a mutation; strains resistant to antibiotics develop over a long time	Mutation is extremely frequent, so that new strains resistant to vaccines emerge in weeks or months
Can live and reproduce in or outside a human or animal host	Can only live and reproduce in the living cells of a host
Can survive (as spores) for very long periods, even centuries	Most die within hours of leaving a host cell if they do not have another cell to live in

NUMBERS AND LETTERS

Flu viruses are divided into three types, called influenza A, B and C. Only type A infects animals as well as humans; types B and C are purely human forms.

Type A flu strains are given names with H and N to show the types of two proteins on their surface. H stands for haemagglutinin and N for neuraminidase. So H5N1 has type-5 haemagglutinin and type-1 neuraminidase. H5N1 is a subtype or strain of A-type influenza. Greatly magnified, the flu virus appears to be a ball covered in spikes and small mushroom shapes. The mushrooms are neuraminidase; the spikes are haemagglutinin.

Although people are most concerned about H5N1 at the moment, other strains can be a threat to us, too. The flu of 1918 was H1N1.

The virus's game plan

To infect your body, a virus has to make its way into a cell and produce copies of itself which it then releases to infect other cells. A virus breaks into a cell by attaching to it – in H5N1, it is the haemagglutinin (the H of the name) that does this part.

Once inside, the virus takes over the cell, forcing it to make copies of the virus's own proteins instead of those the cell needs. It can make 100,000 to one million copies of itself in ten hours. The virus doesn't check the copies it makes, though, and many are defective (mutations). In fact, up to 99 per cent of the copies may be so poor that they can't infect another cell – but that still leaves up to 10,000 viable copies from each infected cell. It's part of the virus's game plan to make defective copies – that is how it mutates to produce different strains that are not recognized by the immune system.

Finally, the copied viruses have to break out of the cell to infect more cells. This is the job of the neuraminidase (the N in the name). The two medicines we have that are effective against bird flu both work because they are neuraminidase inhibitors – they stop the neuraminidase working, so the copied viruses can't get out to spread the infection.

As the flu virus breaks out of a cell, the host cell is destroyed. The dead cells are shed into the lungs, leaving the lungs both denuded of the cells they need to transfer oxygen to the blood, and clogging up with dead matter causing breathing difficulties and coughing.

ATTACK!

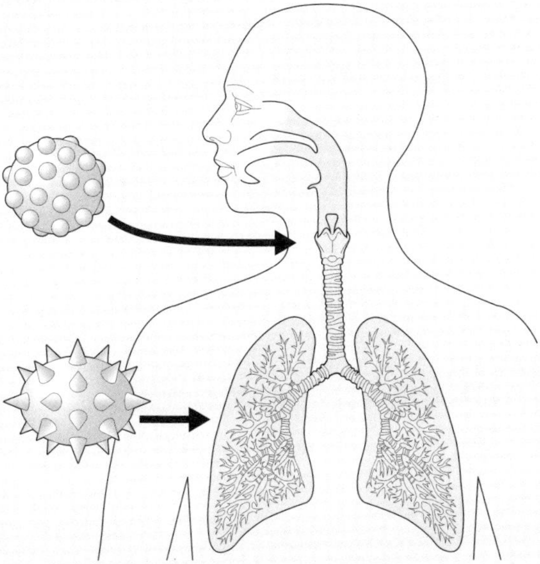

To cause infection, the bird flu virus has to get deep inside a person's lungs. Most flu viruses attack the upper part of the respiratory tract, but the bird flu virus can't attach here. It has to be breathed right in. That's why it is hard to catch. A change in the virus which meant that it could attack further up – the throat or the wider branches of tubes in the lungs – would make it easier to catch, but probably less severe in its effects.

Symptoms can be a good sign!

If the body's immune system recognizes the activity of the virus, it will fight it. Often, it fights off an assault by a virus before you notice you have had any contact with it. If your immune system doesn't recognize the virus, though, the virus gets a chance to spread.

Most of the effects you feel when you are ill are actually caused by your body fighting the infection. A raised temperature, for instance, is a sign that the body is producing more white blood cells to combat disease.

Balancing the books

It is not in the virus's interests to kill people too quickly. A dead person is not breathing out the virus and can't transmit it to other people. Most pandemics kill relatively few of the people they infect. Usually, diseases which are very quickly fatal to most of the people infected die out rapidly – it's simply not possible for them to be passed on easily. The exception is diseases which affect only some of the people infected – some people die while others keep the disease spreading.

For a virus to be successful it must balance spreading widely with killing hosts. If it kills off the whole host population, it will have nowhere to live. Ebola fever is very deadly, killing most of its victims, but it has not spread far. Flu may infect half the world's population, but it kills only a few per cent of those infected.

SUPER-SPREADERS

In the SARS outbreak of 2003, scientists discovered that some people were able to transmit the virus very easily to a huge number of other people. One person passed it to most people in an apartment block he stayed in; another worked in the cabin crew of an airliner and passed it to many passengers. These people were labelled 'super-spreaders', but no one knows why they transmitted the virus so readily.

Return cycles

It is easy to look at the incidence of flu pandemics over the last century and extrapolate some kind of recurrence pattern. But to say that because 1918–57 is a period of 39 years, a pandemic should recur after 39 years is spurious. We could then expect a pandemic in 1996 (overdue) or, counting from the smaller pandemic of 1968, in 2007. But the mutation that will create a pandemic strain of flu is an entirely random event. Over the last three centuries, intervals between flu pandemics have ranged from one year to fifty years.

What is science doing?

Scientists around the world are working to understand how flu viruses change and how they affect the human body. Their research covers the following:

- the structure of flu viruses and the relationships between them
- the characteristics that made the 1918 flu so deadly
- the structure of H5N1 and other flu viruses and what we can tell about how they are changing
- which genes in a flu virus make it transmissible between people and account for human symptoms
- how vaccines can be targeted at the dangerous features of a flu virus
- how we can make flu vaccines more efficiently
- how antiviral drugs can be tailored to new viruses
- how we can manufacture antiviral drugs more efficiently.

At the end of March 2006, scientists in the Netherlands began human trials of a vaccine to counter H5 flu viruses. Although this is not specific to a form of bird flu that may emerge to spread between humans, they hope that it will provide an important starting point for such a vaccine, giving them a head start when – or if – the time comes.

> 'Better a vaccine without an epidemic than an epidemic without a vaccine.'
> *Dr Edward Kilbourne on developing a swine flu vaccine, 1976*

Uncertain future

No one can tell for certain whether or not bird flu will mutate into a form which passes easily between people. If it does change, we do not know yet whether it could retain the severe symptoms that H5N1 from birds has caused in people, or whether it will become much more mild. Many scientists think a pandemic form of H5N1 is likely, but not all agree.

It seems inevitable that a flu pandemic of some type will happen again at some point. There have been plenty in the past and the viruses are still around and evolving. The chances of a pandemic form of H5N1 are hard to assess. Some experts suggest that the chance of a pandemic equivalent to 1918 happening in the next five years may be between one in five and one in ten, and the chances of a much milder pandemic perhaps as high as one in two or one in three. Others say that the 1918 pandemic was a freak, and is much less likely to be repeated.

PANDEMIC NUMBERS

- **Morbidity:** people who fall ill. A morbidity rate of 50 per cent means half the population falls ill. Seasonal flu has a morbidity rate of around 5–10 per cent; pandemic flu usually has a morbidity rate of 25–50 per cent
- **Mortality:** people who die
- **Case mortality rate:** the proportion of ill people who die. A case mortality rate of 2 per cent means 2 per cent of people who contract the illness die. If the morbidity rate is 50 per cent, a case mortality rate of 2 per cent means 1 per cent of the population dies
- **R_0 (reproductive number):** the number of people infected by each infected person. A typical R_0 for flu is around 2 – every infected person passes the disease on to another two people.

The case mortality of seasonal flu is around 0.008 per cent. In 1918, the case mortality in the US was 2.5, meaning that 2.5 per cent of infected people died.

Expert predictions are based on complex mathematical models. They take account of factors including:

- the number of people susceptible to infection
- the number of those likely to be infected (morbidity)
- the proportion of infected people likely to die (case mortality).

In calculating how many people are likely to become infected, they need to look at:

- how easily the illness is transmitted between people (R_0)
- how ill people become
- how long infected people can shed the virus while showing no symptoms themselves
- the proportion of people who can transmit the virus without becoming ill

- the efficacy of treatment or containment measures
- the time of year a pandemic strikes.

If some portions of the population become infected but not ill, they can spread the virus very effectively and make a pandemic much worse.

What then?

> 'The least likely scenario…is the wipeout of a tenth of humanity and the guaranteed collapse of law and order everywhere in the world. Gangs will be running rampant, looting and killing. The cities will become uninhabitable.'
>
> *A. A. Avlicino,* Beat the Flu, *2006*

There are plenty of doom-mongers predicting the total breakdown of society with up to a billion people dead, no essential services and widespread famine. Flu has never caused such widespread devastation, even in 1918, and it seems unlikely that it ever could. In all forms of human transmissible flu that we have known, global case mortality has been relatively low. For one billion people to die, the flu virus would need to infect half the population of the world and kill a third of those infected. It is not impossible, but there is no precedent. The flu virus is not suited to such a scenario.

> 'If the epidemic continues its mathematical rate of acceleration, civilization could easily disappear…from the face of the earth within a matter of a few more weeks.'
>
> *Victor Vaughan, head of the army's Division of Communicable Diseases, writing in 1918*

It is much more likely that we will see the same pattern as in the past – an illness which sweeps the world in two or three waves, incapacitating a lot of people for a week or two at a time and killing a fraction of them. We can expect widespread disruption, economic loss, considerable discomfort and a large number of deaths – but not the end of civilization as we know it.

> 'We do not have to assume that the next pandemic virus, once it appears in a human community, is going to spread rapidly around the world and within a matter of a few weeks cause devastating disease worldwide. This it not the evolution of the pandemics of the 20th century.'
>
> *Dr David Fedson, Medical Director, Vaccines Division, Sanofi-Aventis (retired)*

What are your chances?

Experts disagree about the likelihood of a pandemic striking in the next few years. Some put the chances as high as 70 per cent, others as low as 2 per cent. The following table shows the average chance of death if a pandemic strikes, using different rates of infection and death. In fact, each individual's chance of death will depend on many other factors, including their state of health when infection strikes.

Infection rate	Case mortality	Average chance of death
30%	0.2%	1 in 1,667
50%	0.2%	1 in 1,000
30%	2.5%	1 in 133
50%	2.5%	1 in 80
30%	5%	1 in 67
50%	5%	1 in 40

Total numbers

The World Health Organization (WHO) bases its plans on a pandemic killing 2–7.4 million people; however, it acknowledges that this is a conservative estimate and that it just doesn't know how many people might die. A case mortality of 0.4 per cent would kill 7.4 million people if a third of the world's population was infected. The UK government bases its planning on a pandemic which kills 360,000 people. A case mortality of 2 per cent would kill 360,000 people if 30 per cent of the population was infected. If deaths were evenly spread around the world, which is unlikely, different scenarios give these total death figures:

Infection rate	Case mortality	Total deaths (worldwide)	Deaths US (population 296 million)	Deaths UK (population 60 million)
30%	0.2%	3.6 million	177,600	36,000
50%	0.2%	6 million	296,000	60,000
30%	2.5%	45 million	2.2 million	450,000
50%	2.5%	75 million	3.7 million	750,000
30%	5%	90 million	4.44 million	900,000
50%	5%	150 million	7.4 million	1.5 million

A repeat of the 1918 pandemic, which many experts consider unlikely but some consider quite possible, would give the following figures:

Estimated total deaths 1918	Equivalent portion of current world population	
21.64 million	72 million	1 in 83
48.8 million	163 million	1 in 37
100 million	333 million	1 in 18

These deaths would not be evenly spread over the world; the industrialized west would see the lowest rates, areas of overcrowding in developing nations would see the highest rates.

How fast?

If a pandemic begins, it will probably spread very quickly. The volume of international air traffic means that a virus can spread around the globe in a matter of hours. Experts assess that once the concentration of infection in an area reaches 1 in 10,000 people, spread by air travel is inevitable. This is a guideline – a lower concentration may be needed in an area providing a lot of passengers (such as New York), a higher concentration in an area with less air traffic (such as rural Cambodia).

If a pandemic begins in Thailand, China or Vietnam it is likely to reach Europe and the US in two to four weeks. The pandemic will peak in different areas of the world at different times, taking typically four to six weeks to reach the highest level of infection from the point when it first enters a territory. The spread may be slowed by closing borders and restricting traffic and public gatherings, but the total infection level is unlikely to be reduced, it will just be spread over a longer period. Completely closing borders is not a viable option for most countries in the 21st century, though Iceland did manage to avoid flu in 1918 by closing its borders. Although air and sea traffic could with great difficulty be stopped, land borders are virtually impossible to seal effectively.

Slowing the spread of disease is not pointless. A pandemic stretched over a longer period of time is easier for healthcare services to deal with than one compressed into a shorter period of time. A vaccine will take several months to develop and put into production; if the progress of the disease can be stalled or slowed, there is more chance that a vaccine will be available to help protect some people. Social disruption, though lasting longer, will be less severe if fewer people are sick at the same time. Although the same number of people may ultimately be infected, fewer are likely to die if the pandemic runs more slowly.

How bad?

The effects of flu viruses range from fever, headache, aching muscles and dry cough at the mild end of the spectrum to raging fever, agonizing pain and complications leading to death at the other.

Bird flu in its current form, when contracted by people, has very serious consequences. It may affect not only the lungs but also other body systems, attacking the brain and kidneys in some cases. These effects have been observed in people who have had hospital treatment. We do not know how many people might have been infected but suffered only very minor symptoms which never brought them to the attention of healthcare providers. There is no reason to suppose that all people who have ever been infected with H5N1 have suffered the extreme reaction seen in the hospitalized cases. Indeed, tests carried out on people who have been involved in culling infected flocks have often found the presence of H5N1 antibodies in individuals who have had no symptoms or only mild conjunctivitis (inflammation of the eyes).

H5N1 and AIDS

Around 30 million people in Africa are HIV positive or have AIDS. Their immune system is severely impaired and they will be very vulnerable to any pandemic. The healthcare infrastructure in most sub-Saharan countries is already in a critical state and will be unable to cope with a pandemic. This is one area of the world in which the effects of a pandemic are likely to be brutal and catastrophic – even a relatively mild pandemic could cause many deaths and widespread illness.

Who will be affected?

Flu strikes indiscriminately, but its effects on any individual depend on many factors. Usually, the old and the very young suffer most, along with anyone who has respiratory problems already or an impaired immune system (such as cancer patients, or people who are HIV positive). People with asthma, bronchitis, tuberculosis or any other condition that compromises their lungs are in more danger of serious complications and death than people with sound, healthy lungs.

The 1918 flu pandemic behaved unusually in that most people who died were relatively young and healthy. Males between 20 and 40, and particularly between 25 and 30, were most vulnerable and most likely to die. No one is very sure why this was. It might simply be that people in the prime of life were exposed to the virus most. Troops moving around after the First World War spread the virus quickly, bringing it to their families and friends who were often in the same age group. Another possibility is that one group of the population had natural resistance to the virus, but made effective carriers. By coming into contact with the most socially active group – young and middle-aged adults – they spread it through that part of the population. Many of those who died suffered a cytokine storm response (see p19), and this is most likely to occur in young, healthy people with a robust immune system. The same cytokine storm reaction has been seen in hospitalized patients, who have contracted H5N1 from birds.

In all epidemics and pandemics, there is a close correlation between wealth and mortality levels. Malnutrition lowers resistance to infection by the flu virus itself and to secondary infections, and overcrowding makes for rapid spread and high infection rates.

NO ROOM TO BREATHE

Slum dwellers will be hardest hit. High-density populations with poor sanitary conditions and no access to health care are a tinderbox for epidemic diseases. In the most overcrowded slums of Mumbai, India, the population density is over half a million people per square kilometre. The population density of London is just 4,000 people per square kilometre – less than a hundredth of that in Mumbai. In these slums, the space available for each person is only about ten times the volume of their own body – they cannot possibly avoid breathing in a cocktail of microbes and viruses exhaled by their neighbours.

Living with a pandemic

The world is very different now from the way it was in 1918, or even 1957. The explosion in air travel means that a pandemic virus would spread around the world much more rapidly now than in the past. That does not mean it will kill more people, but that the whole event will be telescoped into a shorter period of time. Perhaps more important in terms of the impact on our lives is the interdependence of different nations. We are heavily dependent on imported fuel, food and consumer goods. We also use more power (gas and electricity), more water and are heavily dependent on telecommunications networks. All this makes us more vulnerable to serious disruption than previous generations.

A pandemic would have an impact on all areas of the workforce, as people took time off sick or just stayed away from work to look after family members or avoid exposure to others. This would affect all sectors, and might have some impact on essential services – not just the electricity supply, but hospitals, schools, public transport, banks, drivers delivering food to supermarkets and staff operating the checkouts. However, many key industries are not labour intensive. It does not take many people to run the power network or the telecommunications industries and it should be possible to keep these going, perhaps with a programme of reduced service.

The WHO estimates that 25–30 per cent of the world's population will fall ill with flu if a pandemic strikes. A pandemic is likely to last several months, with the worst part taking 2–4 months. Not everyone will fall ill at the same time, and many people who are ill will be off work for one or two weeks and then will be fully recovered. Although the effects of this will be disruptive, they do not spell the end of civilization. Possible effects include:

- limited or interrupted deliveries to supermarkets and other shops
- restricted opening hours of shops
- reduced services on public transport
- schools and colleges closed
- public gatherings and sports events cancelled.

The military could be used to help essential services such as the fire brigade, police and ambulance if staff sickness levels in these areas are high. The military may also be drafted to bury the dead.

FAQS

Will there still be electricity, gas and water?

Governments and private organizations will try hard to maintain essential services such as power, gas, telecommunications networks, broadcast (TV and radio). Even so, there may be intermittent cuts, or some services may operate for only a few hours a day during the worst part of the pandemic if it is very severe.

What will happen if the hospitals are full?

All hospitals and healthcare authorities have emergency plans which can quickly be put into action in the event of any disaster, including a pandemic. If necessary, public buildings such as schools may be used as emergency field hospitals. Normal illnesses will not go away during a pandemic, but people might have to accept reduced levels of care and non-urgent treatments will be postponed.

What if there are not enough doctors?

Healthcare services will be severely stretched, not only by the huge burden of extra patient demand, but also by staff being off sick. Retired medical staff may be asked to come back to work, army medical staff may be asked to help in hospitals and some volunteer staff may be used for non-expert aspects of care. As many people as possible will be cared for at home.

Will I have to go to work?

Employers will have their own plans for dealing with a pandemic. Some may encourage teleworking, some may voluntarily close down and others may try to carry on as usual. You might be able to negotiate working from home, or at least change your hours to avoid commuting in packed buses and trains.

Will schools close?

If schools close, the impact on workers in other sectors will be great as many people will need to stay at home to care for children. Governments or local authorities will make decisions about if and when to close schools when a pandemic happens. At the moment, plans say that education authorities will make a decision based on the situation that arises. As children easily pick up and pass on illnesses, you may choose to take your children out of school for the worst part of the pandemic, even if schools remain open.

Pandemic phases

There are six states of pandemic alert. They are:

THE INTERPANDEMIC PERIOD	
Phase 1	No new influenza virus subtypes detected in humans
Phase 2	No new influenza virus subtype detected in humans. Circulating animal influenza virus subtype poses substantial risk of human disease
THE PANDEMIC ALERT PERIOD	
Phase 3	Human infection(s) with a new subtype, but no new human-to-human spread
Phase 4	Small cluster(s) with limited human-to-human transmission
Phase 5	Large cluster(s) but human-to-human spread localized
THE PANDEMIC PERIOD	
Phase 6	Increased and sustained transmission in general population

At the time of writing, we are in stage 3.

Bird flu strikes – phase 6

The following is a fictional scenario showing what might happen if a transmissible strain of bird flu developed. Remember that it is only an illustration. There are many, many other possibilities.

THE HYPOTHETICAL SCENARIO

Day	Date	
1	1 Jan	A poultry worker in Cambodia picks up the H5N1 infection from a diseased chicken
7	7 Jan	A cluster of cases of an unusual illness in an area of Cambodia comes to the attention of health authorities; tests reveal that it is a new strain of H5N1
8	8 Jan	Newspapers worldwide report that a human transmissible form of H5N1 has emerged
11	11 Jan	More clusters emerge in nearby villages and the capital
18	18 Jan	A suspected case is reported in Vietnam
19	19 Jan	200 people are in hospital and 14 are dead; all known contacts of everyone so far infected are treated with antiviral drugs and quarantined
22	22 Jan	Infection runs at 1 in 10,000 of the population of Cambodia
23	23 Jan	Ten cases confirmed in Vietnam
25	25 Jan	Suspected cases reported in Laos and Thailand
30	30 Jan	Confirmed cases in Malaysia, China and Hong Kong; Japan closes its borders for all except essential travel
32	1 Feb	First suspected cases in USA; Australia closes borders for all except essential travel
34	3 Feb	Infection runs at 1 in 10,000 of the population of Vietnam and Laos
40	9 Feb	First confirmed case in Japan
43	12 Feb	Analysis of figures shows a case mortality of 3 per cent with children having a much lower mortality rate; cytokine storm response is main cause of death
44	13 Feb	Very little air traffic as most people refuse to travel; confirmed cases in all areas of the world except Pacific Islands and Australia
49	18 Feb	First suspected cases in Australia
52	21	Confirmed outbreaks in several US cities

59	28 Feb	Tamiflu cuts death rate by 70 per cent in infected cases, but stocks are running out in the Far East; other countries refuse to share stockpiles
60	1 Mar	Infection rate begins to slow in Cambodia
61	2 Mar	Confirmed outbreaks in London, Madrid, Rome, Paris, Berlin
64	5 Mar	Hospitals full in Japan; emergency wards are improvised in schools and sports stadia
65	6 Mar	Confirmed outbreaks in Moscow and Delhi
66	7 Mar	Three people die in USA; panic buying empties supermarkets
69	10 Mar	Panic buying starts in Europe in anticipation of pandemic
81	22 Mar	Schools close and public gatherings banned in all European countries and USA
87	28 Mar	Vaccine announced by US pharmaceutical company but none so far produced
92	2 Apr	600,000 people in UK need hospital treatment, but there are not enough beds
93	3 Apr	Infection rates tailing off in much of the Far East
94	4 Apr	100,000 dead so far in USA; many doctors off sick and some medical supplies exhausted
99	9 Apr	Infection rate starts to drop in USA; deaths still escalating in Europe
110	20 Apr	Death rate begins to drop in USA; infection rate has peaked in Europe
120	30 Apr	Death rate dropping in Europe; vaccine trials begin
139	19 May	Vaccination programmes start, averting a second wave

BIRD FLU AND YOU

Even if H5N1 in birds becomes endemic in Europe and the USA it will never pose a large threat to most people unless a human form emerges. Poultry farmers and people who work with wild birds will adopt appropriate precautions to keep themselves safe, and most of the population has little contact with birds that might be infected. Feeding birds in the garden or park, or visiting wild bird reserves and bird watching, will still be largely safe activities. The threat will be of the same type as that experienced by people who live amongst animals vulnerable to rabies, or in regions where rodents may carry Lyme disease – it will not be an everyday worry.

A strain of bird flu transmissible between people does not yet exist, and it may never exist. But if it does evolve – or if another strain of flu becomes pandemic – there are precautions you can take to help to keep yourself and your family safe.

Be prepared

If a flu pandemic comes, there will be relatively little warning before it reaches every part of the world. Four to six weeks after it starts, most places will probably be affected. This means that once it becomes obvious that a pandemic is starting there will be little time to prepare. Your priorities for yourself and your family must be:

- to avoid infection
- to have sufficient supplies if you are ill, or if there is disruption in deliveries to shops
- to look after yourself and your family if anyone falls ill.

The time to make sure you have adequate supplies is well in advance. Panic buying is almost inevitable. The more people who are better prepared and don't need to buy at the last minute, the better for everyone.

Drugs

Only two existing antiviral medicines have had any effect on the human H5N1 infections in the Far East – Tamiflu and Relenza. Some restistance even to these has been reported and there is no guarantee at all that they will be effective against a new strain of H5N1 transmissible between people.

Tamiflu®

- Tamiflu is the trade name under which oseltamivir is sold. It is made only by the Swiss pharmaceutical giant Roche, but may soon be made under licence in some developing countries.
- It has been available to combat winter flu since 1998.
- Unlike most other antiflu medicines, Tamiflu is effective to some extent in treating H5N1, but it is not a cure.
- It can reduce the symptoms and the chance of serious complications, but it may not prevent or reduce the spread of flu.
- It is a neuraminidase inhibitor – it works by blocking the mechanism the virus uses to break out of cells it has infected, so preventing it infecting more cells.
- Tamiflu is provided in capsules which are swallowed.
- It must be taken within a couple of days of the onset of symptoms to have any effect, and two 75mg tablets a day are needed for five days. To avoid developing flu after exposure to it, one tablet a day is taken for at least seven days. It cannot be taken by pregnant women or babies under one year old.
- Governments around the world are stockpiling Tamiflu as it is currently the best we have. Roche is making Tamiflu as fast as possible but it will take many months to fill the backlog of orders from around the world.
- Some large corporations, particularly in the US, have been buying up Tamiflu in the hope of protecting their workforce (and so their economic interests) during a pandemic. Roche has now stopped supplying Tamiflu to private organizations and is dealing only with orders from governments and healthcare bodies.
- It is estimated that 90 per cent of the Tamiflu produced will go to wealthy countries, which so far have least need of it.
- In October 2005 Roche refused to relax its patent so that other companies could produce Tamiflu and increase the available supply. Roche is negotiating sharing parts of the production process with some poorer countries to reduce costs for

countries that need large supplies but cannot afford them.

- Roche aims to produce 400 million Tamiflu treatments a year and has a backlog of orders from around the world. There is no guarantee that Tamiflu would work against a version of H5N1 transmissible between people. Bird flu in Vietnam has already shown some resistance to Tamiflu, and resistance could become widespread.
- The UK has ordered enough Tamiflu to treat 25 per cent of the population, though it has not yet all been delivered.

Relenza®

- Relenza is the trade name under which zanamivir is sold. It is made only by Glaxo Wellcome Inc.
- It has been available to combat winter flu since 1999.
- It is effective to some extent in treating H5N1, but it is not a cure.
- It can be used to treat flu, but not to prevent it or prevent its spread to other people.
- It is a neuraminidase inhibitor – it works by blocking the mechanism the virus uses to break out of cells it has infected, so preventing it infecting more cells.
- Relenza is provided as a powder which is inhaled using a special inhaler.
- It must be taken within a couple of days of the onset of symptoms to have any effect, and must be inhaled twice a day for five days. It cannot be used by pregnant women or children under seven years old.
- As Relenza is more difficult to use than Tamiflu it is not being stockpiled as enthusiastically as Tamiflu in most countries, but the US is keeping large supplies.
- There is no guarantee that Relenza would work against a version of H5N1 transmissible between people. Some resistance to Relenza has already been found and it could become widespread.

Should you buy Tamiflu?

It is not possible to buy Tamiflu over the counter in a pharmacy – it is a prescription-only drug. You will be very unlikely to find a doctor willing to prescribe Tamiflu for you now – it won't be prescribed as a preventive, and you would only be likely to get it if you knew you had been exposed to H5N1.

There is a thriving black market in Tamiflu – or tablets that are claimed to be Tamiflu – on the Internet. Only you can decide whether you want to risk buying these. Some considerations to bear in mind are:

- The price of Tamiflu on the black market is very high, and there is no guarantee that what you are buying is really Tamiflu.
- If you buy something which is not genuine Tamiflu and take it, it may do you no good and could even cause you harm. If you take it instead of seeking other treatment, you could leave time for complications to set in before you get effective medical care.
- Tamiflu is desperately needed in countries where H5N1 is already a problem. This situation can only be made worse by people stockpiling it when they don't need it.
- Using Tamiflu to avoid contracting flu, you would need to take it every day for the duration of a pandemic. There are ten capsules in a course of Tamiflu, so for one person to take a capsule a day for three months would need 90 capsules, or nine packs.
- If you take it just when you get flu, you will need at least one or two courses.

Alternative remedies

Whenever there is a pandemic of any disease, alternative and often bogus remedies are touted enthusiastically. They range from mainstream alternative therapies through folk remedies to the downright bizarre:

- **Oscillococcinum:** homeopathic remedy recommended for the treatment of flu, extracted from the heart and liver of the Barbary duck
- **elderberry cordial/syrup/tea:** elderberry is a traditional English folk remedy for flu
- **kimchi:** Korean fermented cabbage with radishes, ginger, garlic and red peppers. An extract of kimchi is claimed to have

some effect treating H5N1 in birds

- **Echinacea:** traditional herbal remedy for flu
- **Gan Mao Ling:** traditional Chinese remedy for flu, best taken after exposure to the disease and before the onset of symptoms.

Vaccine, what vaccine?

When a pandemic strain of flu emerges, pharmaceutical companies will race to produce a vaccine. This will involve isolating the strain of flu, using reverse genetic engineering to discover its genetic code, reproducing it with the dangerous aspects disabled, culturing the safe version and then growing a supply using fertilized chicken eggs. The whole process is likely to take somewhere between four and six months.

The current way of growing a vaccine, in chicken eggs, cannot be rushed. It may also run into problems as H5N1 has been found to kill the fertilized eggs. If the pandemic strain did this, it would not be possible to produce a vaccine using the usual method. Cell culture is a possible alternative, but there has not been sufficient exploration of, and investment in, this method for a large-scale operation to be set up quickly. Once working, however, it could produce a vaccine more quickly than the egg method.

The Food and Drug Administration (FDA) in the US has refused to consider fast-tracking approval for a new flu vaccine. All countries have their own approval procedures, though, so the US decision will not affect people elsewhere. It is likely that some countries with less rigorous regulations will approve a vaccine more quickly, probably sparking a global black market in vaccines not available in some western countries.

If an effective vaccine does become available, different countries will set different criteria for its use. There are competing goals in deciding who should have the vaccine:

- reducing deaths (giving it to vulnerable people)
- reducing disease (giving it to people who come into contact with many others)
- limiting the impact of the pandemic (giving it to key workers)
- ensuring essential services (giving it to key workers)
- equitable distribution (giving everyone an equal chance).

It is likely that in most places, healthcare workers will have the first doses of vaccine. Thereafter, some countries may give it to the military; others may choose key workers in essential industries; some may go to senior government officials and those involved in broadcasting (in order to keep mass communication channels operating).

Before we have a vaccine for the pandemic strain, scientists are producing a vaccine for H5N1 in its current form. Many countries are ordering this now in the hope that it will give at least some protection to health workers before a specific vaccine becomes available.

We can't depend on a vaccine being ready in time before a pandemic strikes, but it may protect people from a second or third wave of infection. It is worth trying to avoid infection for as long as possible – you might get the vaccine in the end!

Keep yourself safe

Flu is transmitted between people in droplets that are exhaled (breathed out) or ejected more forcefully by coughing and sneezing. Sneezing can send 100,000 virus particles shooting across the room at 167 km per hour and they can be carried over a distance of five metres. Another person can become infected if they breathe in these droplets, or if the droplets fall on a person's eyes or lips. Most droplets quickly fall out of the air and don't travel more than about one to two metres (three to six feet). Instead, they fall onto surfaces, or onto another person's skin. The most common way of becoming infected is by transferring viral particles to the mouth or eyes on your own hands.

Survival of flu virus	
On skin	A few minutes
On a soft or porous surface	6–8 hours
On a hard surface	24–48 hours

The single most effective way of cutting the risk of catching flu is to wash your hands frequently with hot water and soap. If there is no access to hot water and soap, use alcohol-based hand wipes or gel.

Handwashing

- Wet your hands with warm water
- Use plenty of soap or handwash
- Rub all over your hands, including between the fingers, the ends of fingers and particularly the thumbs, the knuckles, wrists and lower arms
- Rinse all the soap off
- Dry your hands very thoroughly, preferably with a paper towel or a hot-air hand drier. At home, make sure towels are kept dry as damp towels make a better environment for germs to survive.

Make sure children are proficient at proper handwashing.

Because the flu virus can survive longest on hard surfaces, it is important to clean surfaces frequently with an antiviral or alcohol-based cleaner. In particular, clean:

- handles of doors, cupboards and drawers
- lavatory flush, lavatory seat and taps
- doors of cookers, fridges and cupboards
- tables, work surfaces
- light switches, phones, computer keyboard and mouse, remote controls
- toys, and especially those which babies might put into their mouths.

Cleaning household objects and surfaces is especially important if someone in the house is ill. When you are out and about, remember that other people may have left viruses on shop doors, the handles of shopping trolleys and baskets, ATMs, vending machines, handrails on trains and buses – almost anywhere. You can't avoid touching these, but you can be rigorous about washing your hands and making sure that you don't touch your face or eat after touching surfaces and before you wash. It can be useful to make children wear woollen gloves whenever they are out of the house – gloves won't protect them from the virus, but it's hard to bite your nails or eat in gloves, so it will serve as a reminder. Insist that as soon as they take the gloves off, for whatever reason, they wash their hands. Remember the gloves will be contaminated; wash them often and don't put them on surfaces where they can release their load of viruses.

It's not only people who are obviously ill who may pose a threat. Many illnesses, including flu, can be transmitted to others before the person with the disease feels at all ill. And between 30 and 50 per cent of people who are asymptomatic – who have a disease but never fall ill with it – pass it on to other people.

Bird flu masks – do they work?

Opinion is divided about whether masks work, or whether they might even put you at greater risk of catching flu. There are several types of mask.

The disposable masks that we saw many people wearing during the SARS outbreak of 2003 are made of gauze or paper and have no security rating. Whether or not they actually stop any virus particles is debatable.

Graded masks are labelled FFP2 or FFP3 in the UK, N95 or N99 in Europe. They should stop 95 per cent and 99 per cent of particles respectively. However, they must fit properly and be used properly.

Masks with a valve offer the best security. They may stop you breathing in droplets carrying a virus, but they do not stop you breathing them out and infecting other people if you are already infected. They also hamper breathing, so you will need a break from wearing one.

Most masks do not stop the smallest particles, and it is those that are the most dangerous. Larger droplets and particles that carry a virus generally fall to the ground quite quickly and do not remain airborne for you to breathe in, but these are the ones stopped by most masks. Smaller droplets and particles are small enough to pass through the mask anyway. These are the particles that can penetrate most deeply into your lungs and so are the most dangerous.

Some people believe that a mask offers false security and may increase your risk by encouraging you to feel safe. There is also a danger of transferring viral particles to your hands while removing the mask. The UK government's advice does not recommend that most people use masks. On the other hand, the French government is stockpiling masks. It may be worth keeping masks if you have a small child or baby, so that you can wear a mask near them and prevent breathing over them too much and risk infecting them.

Most people, too, will probably not dispose of masks safely after use but will be tempted to re-use them, increasing the risk of picking up viruses from a used mask. A virus can live on the fabric part of a mask for around eight hours and on the hard plastic for longer.

If you do decide to use a flu mask, make sure you research the best available to you (look for FFP3 or N99, or masks with a valve). Burn masks after use if possible, and always wash your hands after touching or removing a used mask.

Keeping safe while nursing a sick person

If someone in your household falls sick, you will need to be especially careful to avoid infection. It is not inevitable that if one person falls ill everyone else will; about 21 per cent of people living in the same house as a person infected with ordinary flu contract the disease. By being rigorous with hygiene, you may still keep yourself well.

- Use disposable gloves when handling a sick person, their used tissues and anything they have touched.
- Wash your hands every time you touch a sick person or enter their room.
- Clean all surfaces thoroughly and frequently.
- Wash any bedclothes or sheets at a high temperature.
- Use antiviral tissues and don't touch soiled tissues. Wash your hands after throwing the tissues away.
- If possible, turn away from the person, especially while they cough or sneeze.
- If you have masks, use one while tending a sick person.

Plan, don't panic

> 'We should be worried but not panicked.'
> *Dr Andrew Pavia, Chairman of the Infectious Disease Society of America's Pandemic Influenza Task Force*

To survive a pandemic as comfortably as possible takes planning and preparation. The time to do that is now, while you can think clearly and calmly and weigh up different possibilities without the urgency that a pandemic will bring. This is also the time to equip yourself with basic supplies, before there are shortages as people panic buy and while you can spread the cost.

Staying in

If a pandemic strikes, you should aim first to avoid infection. The best way of avoiding infection is to avoid spending time with people who might be infected or in places where infected people may have shed the virus. This will mean staying away from people other than your own family as much as possible. Your workplace may be closed down; schools and colleges may be closed. Even if they are not, you may plan to work or study from home and to enable your children to be educated at home.

If you can work from home, or even avoid busy commuter buses and trains, you will cut down the chances of becoming ill. Also cut down trips to the shops by buying as much as you can each time, and buying in advance.

Some people plan to shut themselves in their houses for the duration of a pandemic. If you are able to do this, it will certainly help your chance of avoiding illness. It needs careful planning and preparation. You will need to make sure you have adequate supplies in your home to avoid having to make trips out to the shops.

Quarantine

Quarantine is a period of isolation to help prevent the spread of a disease. It is unlikely that quarantine will be imposed on people in the west, though some Far Eastern countries are including quarantining of some residential areas or entire villages in their pandemic plans. Compulsory quarantine will be difficult to impose, but at times of high infection rates you may be asked to stay indoors as much as possible.

DID YOU KNOW?

The word quarantine comes from the Italian word 'quarante' meaning 'forty'. The original period of quarantine was forty days, imposed during times of plague.

If you or members of your household fall sick with flu, you will probably not feel well enough to go out. But you should, in any case, stay inside and avoid contact with other people. Even if you seem well, you may be able to pass on the virus to other people. The impact of an epidemic will be worse if people do not take care to contain the illness.

Emergency stock

If you are going to stay in the house while you are ill, or for a longer period, you will need supplies. Don't depend on being able to order food from the supermarket online – if lots of people are ill, delivery systems may well breakdown. It's far better to have supplies that you can draw on if you need them. Build up a stock slowly, so that you can spread the cost.

If you are planning to spend the whole pandemic period locked in your house, you will need many more supplies than if you just want to prepare for a period of illness. It will take a lot more planning – and remember that all these supplies take a lot of space, too. Your stockpile will need to include:

- food and water
- disinfectant and cleaning supplies
- medicines and essential toiletries
- emergency equipment such as matches, torch, batteries.

Food

Choose non-perishable foods such as dry rice, pasta and pulses, dried fruit and tinned foods. You might keep extra supplies in the freezer, but don't depend on these – if the electricity supply is cut off at any time you may lose it all. Include plenty of foods that you can eat without cooking in case the gas or electricity supply is interrupted.

Begin by deciding how long you want your supplies to last. If you are planning to stay in for the duration of a pandemic, a minimum of two months is sensible. If you have space to store and money to buy food for four months, that is best. But anything at all is better than nothing. To spread the cost, plan what you will need and buy it slowly, perhaps one or two items on each shopping trip if you shop daily, or several things each time if you shop weekly.

Working out what you need

There are different ways of working out how much food to keep and what kinds. One way is to base it on the calorie requirements of your family.

How many calories a week?

Adult woman*	14,000
Adult man	17,500
Young child	10,500
Older child	As adults

*A pregnant or breast-feeding woman will need more calories than this. Bear this in mind if you are planning pregnancy.

Don't aim just to have enough calories. To keep yourself healthy and give your immune system the best chance of fighting any infections, you need to maintain your intake of vitamins and minerals, and keep a sensible balance of protein, fibre, carbohydrate and fat. Use the Internet or a book on nutrition to help you plan meals you will enjoy that will give you a healthy, nutritional balance.

You may prefer to plan meals for a few days or a week, work out what you will need to make them and then multiply by the number of weeks you want to prepare for. If you do this, keep your list of meals and what they contain with your stockpile so that other people can see how to use your supplies to get the best benefit from them.

	Good source of	How long will it keep?
Tinned fruit and vegetables	Vitamins and fibre	1–2 years
Dried fruit	Fibre, carbohydrates, vitamins	1 year
Nuts	Protein, essential oils	3 months
Tinned fish	Essential oils, protein	2–3 years
Tinned meat (and meat products)	Protein	2–3 years
Rice, pasta, noodles	Protein, carbohydrates	2–3 years

Yeast, flour to make bread, chapattis, etc	Carbohydrates	1 year
Long-life milk	Protein	3–6 months
Long-life fruit juices	Vitamins	9 months
Vacuum-packed meals		Variable
Breakfast cereals	Carbohydrates, fibre, vitamins	1 year
Dried or tinned beans, lentils, peas	Protein, fibre, vitamins	1–2 years

Don't forget cooking oil, or lard if you use it.

There is nothing wrong with including some biscuits and other treats once you have met your dietary needs, especially if they will help keep your spirits up. But don't depend on them for your calorie intake as they have little nutritional value, and if you have limited storage space they should be the things to drop. Store long-life fruit juice rather than fizzy drinks and alcohol – it's a better use of space and money.

If you drink coffee, tea or herbal infusions, keep these, too – the more normal your life, the happier and healthier you are likely to be. For the same reason, include bottled sauces, dried herbs and spices and other flavourings you use so that your food is as pleasant as possible.

Keep it up-to-date

There is no guarantee that a flu pandemic will happen this winter, or next winter. It may not come for five years, or perhaps even longer. Although some of your supplies will stay in good condition for several years, others will get stale. Check your stockpile every three months or so, and take out anything that will go out of date in the next three months to use, replacing it with exactly the same quantity.

Remember that your stockpile is good for any emergency, not just a flu pandemic. If you are ill and can't get out, or if a natural disaster such as flooding or blizzards isolates your home, the stockpile will be invaluable. Just remember to replace whatever you use as soon as you can.

Water

The water supply is unlikely to be affected by a pandemic. However, if you are worried, buy several large plastic containers of mineral water. The type used in water dispensers is suitable. You should view this as essential drinking water only – you won't have enough space to store water for washing, flushing the toilet and so on. Allow at least two litres of water a day for each person in your household.

Not just food

You don't only need food to keep you going through a pandemic. Cleaning will be very important, especially if anyone in your household falls ill.

Use the checklist below to make sure you have everything you will need.

- ☐ Soap, washing-up liquid and washing powder/liquid. Hygiene is important – don't skimp on these
- ☐ Disposable nappies, sanitary towels or tampons, contraceptive supplies, incontinence pads
- ☐ Toothpaste, toothbrushes, shampoo and other essential toiletries
- ☐ Alcohol-based hand wipes or gel, disinfectant, disposable plastic gloves, protective masks – for tending to anyone who falls sick
- ☐ Pet food
- ☐ Light bulbs, matches, candles, wind-up torch
- ☐ Batteries for torches, smoke detectors, hearing aids and less essential items like personal stereos and electronic games
- ☐ Wind-up or battery-operated radio for hearing the news if there are power outages
- ☐ Prescription and regular medicines – if anyone in the family is on regular medication for an ongoing condition such as high blood pressure, heart disease, asthma, eczema, diabetes or epilepsy, make sure you have several months' supply
- ☐ Basic medicines for colds, seasonal flu, headaches, period pain, minor injuries, stings, bites, etc. Normal life and normal afflictions won't go away during a pandemic
- ☐ Medicines for flu infection – although you can't cure flu, you can make yourself feel better by alleviating some of the

symptoms with paracetamol-based or other flu remedies (don't give aspirin-based medicines to children under 12)

- ☐ Digital strip thermometers and alcohol-based wipes to clean them, rehydration salts, anti-viral tissues
- ☐ Things to do – several months in the house is a long time. Keep some books you haven't read (the longer the better!) DVDs and music, plenty of paper and pencils/pens, puzzle books and anything else you might want to amuse yourself.

BOREDOM MAKES BABIES

Much of Britain suffered extensive power shortages in the 1970s and people spent many long, dark evenings with no TV; the birth rate rose considerably nine months later. When people are bored, they have sex. Make sure you have a good supply of contraceptives – the middle of a pandemic is not the time to seek antenatal care.

Keep it safe

Find a good place to store your supplies. They need to be:

- at a stable temperature, preferably fairly cool but not somewhere they could be damaged by frost
- dry – protect them from rain, surface water, damp and humidity
- safe from insect and rodent pests.

Sturdy plastic boxes with close-fitting lids will protect from pests and damp. You might keep your boxes in the attic, garage or a shed to start with, but bring them indoors at the first sign of a pandemic. You don't want to have to brave bad weather and haul heavy boxes in if you are feeling ill.

Prepare at least one box, clearly labelled, with everything you will need if you are ill. Make sure it has medical supplies and food that is easy to eat and nutritious. Keep this box easily accessible and make sure everyone in your family knows where it is. Keeping an emergency box to hand is particularly important if you live alone.

Sick room

Although you will hope to keep yourself and your family free from infection, you may not be lucky. Plan and equip a sick room so that you are well prepared if you do need it. When choosing a room to use as a sick room, look for:

- a bed that is easily accessible all round so that you can tend to the patient's needs easily
- ventilation: getting frequent changes of air is important to reduce the concentration of virus in the room
- near a toilet: patients may not always be well enough to get up to go to the toilet, but when they are well enough, it should be as short a trip as possible
- easily controlled heating: it's important to keep the patient comfortable
- pleasant surroundings: avoid harsh lighting, and attempt to have a TV or radio in the room. At their worst, the patient may not want either of these, but the worst part of flu lasts only a couple of days and after that they will be bored
- a method of calling for help: it can be a baby alarm, a gong, a mobile phone or an intercom – even a child's drum or a bicycle bell. But remember a person with flu may not have the breath to call loudly or the energy to move much.

Have a supply of tissues, disposable rubber gloves, disinfectant spray, medicines to relieve symptoms and a thermometer all ready in the room. Make sure you know where to find blankets and basic medicines.

Antiviral tissues are best. They will not cure you of flu or even a cold, but antiviral chemicals in them will work to kill viruses in the liquid sneezed or coughed into them, reducing the risks to other people who come into contact with the used tissues. It takes around 15 minutes for the antiviral chemicals to work, so don't touch used tissues until some time has passed. Make sure anyone looking after a sick person washes their hands frequently, even if antiviral tissues are used.

It is better to nurse sick people in separate rooms rather than putting them together, but this is not always possible. Try to screen patients from one another if they have to be in the same room. It is, undoubtedly, better not to share a room with a sick patient, but where sick children are involved you may feel that you would rather stay with them.

When the sick person has recovered, clean everything in the room thoroughly with disinfectant and leave the room to air for a couple of days if at all possible.

Remember, you may be the one to fall sick. Don't depend on being able to put your plans into action yourself – write up a proper plan and list of items and where they are stored so that someone else can work with your preparations if necessary.

Looking after a sick patient

If a pandemic starts, official guidelines will be issued to help you look after someone sick with flu at home. The guidelines will also explain when to call for expert medical help. The information will be made widely available and will probably be delivered to each house in the country.

Whenever you are nursing a sick person, you need to protect your own well-being as well as looking after the patient. You will not be able to nurse them if you become ill yourself, so don't cut corners or take risks with hygiene.

A sick person needs to be kept warm, but not uncomfortably hot, and must have enough fluids. They may not want food, but you should offer foods that are high in liquid and easy to eat. Fluids are much more important than solid food. You will need to monitor the person's temperature and do what you can to keep them comfortable. Practise using your digital thermometer on someone now if you are not used to using it.

If you live alone

You need to be particularly careful with your preparations if you live alone. Decide who you will call on for help if you fall ill and agree it with them. Make sure you have all the supplies you may need, including food that is very easy to prepare and eat – you may only be able to nibble on biscuits and sip water, but make sure they are available.

At the first sign of illness, put your preparations into practice, bringing in anything you have stored in a shed or garage and making sure everything will be as easy as possible for the days while you are ill. Have someone who will check on you daily, or who you can call by phone daily at a pre-arranged time.

Don't panic

> 'We can't make this pandemic go away, because it is a natural phenomenon, it will come. But what we can do is to limit its impact.'
> *Sir Liam Donaldson, UK Chief Medical Officer*

Disease used to strike from nowhere – unexpected, terrifying and incomprehensible. Now, for the first time in human history, we have good warning that a pandemic may be about to sweep the planet. We know where the disease may come from, roughly how it works and even how we may be able to fight it, given time to get our defences in order. We are better equipped than ever before to meet the challenge. Each of us in the industrialized world has the information and resources to prepare ourselves to some degree, and in doing so we have a chance to lessen the impact of a pandemic for ourselves and society. For our task is not just to look after ourselves as individuals and our own families, but to look out for others too. In 1918, ignorance and fear led people to leave their sick neighbours to starve to death. Fear became as great a threat as disease.

> 'A society that takes as its motto, "every man for himself" is no longer a civilized society.'
> *John M. Barry,* The Great Influenza, *2005*

Bird flu may never produce a pandemic, or it may prove a damp squib, fizzling around the world in mild coughs and sneezes. If so, we will have been lucky. But having been prepared will have done no harm, and will equip us to deal more easily with the next pandemic, for it will surely come one day.

PANDEMIC PLAN

Fill in essential details of your own pandemic planning. Make sure everyone in your household knows about the plans you have made, and where you are keeping this book so that they can look at your list if they need to. Remember that if you are ill yourself, someone else may need to use your plan and your supplies. Have you:

- ☐ Prepared a written plan?
- ☐ Stored food?
- ☐ Noted recipes or meal plans for your food store?
- ☐ Stored hygiene supplies and medicines?
- ☐ Stored basic essentials, such as torch and radio?
- ☐ Prepared a box with a week's emergency supplies in case you are ill?

Where are your supplies kept? ______________________

Where have your stored:

Food? ______________________

Hygiene basics and medicines? ______________________

Basic essentials? ______________________

Your emergency box? ______________________

If you have the following, where are they stored?

Tamiflu ______________________

Flu masks ______________________

Where is your written plan kept? ______________________

Essential contacts

Who should be contacted if you fall ill?

Name ______________ Phone number ______________

Who is your doctor?

Name ______________ Phone number ______________

Who do you need to keep in touch with, to check whether they need help, if a pandemic strikes?

Name ______________ Phone number ______________

List the medicines taken regularly by all members of your household. This information may be needed in a hurry if you seek medical attention in an emergency.

Name ______________ Medicine ______________

Name ______________ Medicine ______________

Name ______________ Medicine ______________

FURTHER INFO

Scientific and practical

www.newscientist.com/channel/health/bird-flu
Up-to-date information on the current situation and links to pages covering the scientific background of H5N1 in birds and people

www.who.int/csr/disease/influenza/pandemic10things/en/
Information on pandemics
World Health Organization

www.cdc.gov/flu/avian/
Extensive information about the science of bird flu, the current situation and guidance for travellers
Center for Disease Control, US

Current situation

www.defra.gov.uk/animalh/diseases/notifiable/disease/ai/
Information from Defra on the current situation in Britain, with photos and descriptions of symptoms to look for in domestic poultry and current advice on dealing with poultry and wild birds, including what to do if you find a dead bird
Department for Environment, Food and Rural Affairs, UK

www.cdc.gov/flu/avian/outbreaks/current.htm
Information on outbreaks of H5N1
Center for Disease Control and Prevention
www.who.int/csr/disease/avian_influenza/country/cases_table_20

06_04_12/en/
Table showing number of human cases of H5N1 and deaths by year for different countries, updated weekly
World Health Organization

Pandemic contingency plans

www.dh.gov.uk/pandemicflu
Link to UK government contingency plans for a flu pandemic and advice for travellers
Department of Health, UK

www.phac-aspc.gc.ca/influenza/pandemicplan_e.html
Canadian pandemic influenza plan
Public Health Agency of Canada

www.whitehouse.gov/homeland/pandemic-influenza.html
Contingency pandemic plan for the US
Homeland Security Council, US

INDEX